Tobey Gross

UN-HELP

Why Your Pain Is Profitable
An Epistemic Critique of the
Self-Help Industry

MINKOWSKI
Institute Press

Dr. Tobey Gross
Professor of Educational Science
www.tobeygross.de

ISBN: 978-1-998902-68-2 (softcover)
ISBN: 978-1-998902-69-9 (ebook)

Minkowski Institute Press
Montreal, Quebec, Canada
https://minkowskiinstitute.com/mip/

For information on all Minkowski Institute Press publications
visit our website at https://minkowskiinstitute.com/mip/books/

CONTENTS

To Juliane and Matthias.
This is very much not a book on parenting.

ACKNOWLEDGEMENTS

Having Stephen Turner as a reader and reviewer of this work is a privilege I value deeply. Your approval affirms its merit and strengthens my confidence in it. Thank you for taking the time and the kind review.

I would like to thank Fanny Guglielmucci for discussions that have truly enriched my perspectives far beyond this work. The depth of your insights is not only inspirational but also moving on a deep level.

I am also expressing deep gratitude toward Vesselin Petkov for reviewing this work and being so supportive, reliable and kind in this, *and former*, publication processes. It is my honor to work with you.

PREFACE

In the age of algorithmic influence and instant inspiration, a billion-dollar market has emerged around the promise of personal transformation. Each week unveils a new bestseller, a viral clip, a charismatic coach – all offering distilled blueprints for success, happiness, and psychological wellbeing. Become productive. Think positively. Master your morning. Heal your trauma in five steps. From nutritional hacks to emotional detoxes, the self-help and mindset economy has become a cultural engine that speaks in the language of healing, while operating under the logic of performance, scalability, and return on investment.

But why, after such exhaustive engagement with these solutions, does the sense of lack persist? Why, even after meticulous self-tracking, relentless optimization, and immersion in curated routines, do many individuals find themselves no closer to clarity, peace, or meaningful selfunderstanding? What appears on the surface as a pluralism of empowering strategies reveals itself, under scrutiny, to be a homogenized ideology: a system of affective capitalism that transforms suffering into sales, and existential discontent into perpetual demand.

This work offers a critical-epistemological inquiry into that system. It treats the self-help industry not merely as a cultural curiosity or commercial trend, but as a psychopolitical formation – one that appropriates the language of psychological care while instrumentalizing vulnerability for economic and ideological ends. The core thesis is that the modern self-help ethos does not alleviate suffering but re-frames content-

ment as deficiency (Ehrenreich, 2009). Its deepest function
is not to empower, but to generate recursive inadequacy: a
state of chronic self-surveillance, internalized pressure, and
moralized failure.

At the heart of this cycle is a set of unspoken assump-
tions: that happiness is a choice, that fulfillment is a product, that mental health is a function of mindset (Cabanas &
Illouz, 2019). This logic reconfigures the terrain of psychology – from an open exploration of inner life to a prescriptive
regimen of optimization. It converts the existential condition
into a solvable algorithm, repackaging complex psychological
realities into neatly consumable aphorisms. The result is not
therapeutic engagement but motivational conditioning, not
clinical insight but affective manipulation.

Methodologically, this work takes its stance in the tradition of reflective, theory-based psychological inquiry. It is
not an empirical study, nor does it present statistical find-
ings or experimental data. Its foundation lies instead in clinical knowledge, conceptual reasoning, and epistemological critique. Drawing from psychodynamic theory, philosophical
psychology, existential thought, and cultural discourse analysis, this monograph pursues a hermeneutic approach to psychological culture – one that seeks to uncover how suffering is
framed, narrated, and commodified in the 'modern psyche'.

The approach is integrative and interpretive: it treat texts,
slogans, digital performances, and guru rhetoric not as anec-
dotal curiosities but as artifacts of a deeper epistemic structure. This is psychology not reduced to behavior or numbers, but expanded toward meaning, narrative, and symbolic
depth. It is an approach shaped by an understanding of the
human mind as fundamentally conflicted, layered, and situated – not as a system to be fixed, but a life to be understood.

What follows is not a how-to manual, but a philosophical
psychology of the self-help condition. It is a conceptual car-
tography of epistemic distortion, motivational pseudowisdom,
and the commodification of psychic life. It aims to reclaim the
space of psychological reflection from the imperatives of mar-

ket logic, and to re-center complexity, depth, and narrative integrity at the heart of our understanding of healing.

4

INTRODUCTION

Note on terminology: In this work, self-help and mindset industry / economy and self-help and mindset culture are used interchangeably. I consider both terms appropriate for the description since on the one hand, it is an industry with monetary motives and market logic, but on the other hand also a culture-like formation and operation.

In contemporary landscapes, psychological discourse is no longer existent solely in clinics, universities and among professionals or academic journals. It has long been adopted and subsumed into the fabric of the digital economy, where emotional states and subjective perception and struggle are rendered marketable assets (Zuboff, 2019). The internet with its boundless platforms of selfexpression has given rise to a new form of *emotional consumerism* where affect is no longer simply experienced but rather curated, displayed and monetized.

Human suffering can be increasingly seen as content, while simultaneously, creators on platforms position themselves as the arbiters of salvation and relief. Emotional experiences are captured and formatted and algorithmically amplified based on their capacity to engage, seduce and retain attention. In a broader perspective, that means the suffering individual subject is encouraged to narrate their pain in ways that are digestible, optimizable, *profitable*. This shift is not incidental by any means. It reflects a profound epistemic mutation: psychology itself, stripped of its reflective and clinical dimensions, is refashioned as an instrument of consumer culture. Emotional struggles are transformed into content niches, where mental health advice becomes a viral branding; resilience, authenticity, vulnerability become lifestyle. Psychological inquiry, in its traditional aim of understanding the nature of inner conflict and accompany the subject through existential suffering, guard transformation, is displaced by the imperatives of sales conversion (cf. 'affective capitalism'; Illouz, 2008).

This drives one market logic: the more intense and persistent the insecurity, the more vibrant and attractive the market for its relief. Its *potential* relief, that is. Emotional consumerism ensures that suffering is never resolved for it fuels a cycle of content production, consumption and residual dissatisfaction – a cycle which every click, share, and every 'motivational intervention' sustains the malaise it pretends to heal. Psychological wisdom is now reduced to consumable spectacle, compressed into optimized affirmations, curated soundbites. The complexity of psychological suffering in its individual inquiry and existential humility is hollowed out and refashioned into a series of generic slogans, disseminated en masse across social media platforms. This rise of 'instant wisdom' on TikTok, Instagram, YouTube and similar spaces reflects a profound epistemological degradation of psychological discourse.

Not only is this antithetical to the spirit of authentic psychological inquiry. But also it neglects the fact that traditional clinical psychology recognizes that suffering is irreducibly particular and needs a ground where subjective histories are carefully unfolded. The intersection of personal biography, unconscious conflict, social circumstance, existential condition, is turned into the very opposite in self-help and mindset industries. It delivers generalized, flattened and universalized formulas, operates on faulty premises that psychic pain can simply be categorized and addressed with prescripted immediate relief-interventions. This reveals the logical flaw of the very mode of communication: with no inquiry and no interest in an individual's life world, no reflection on contextual realities, how are these pieces of advice, these one-size-fits-all explanations *not* pseudosolutions? Where the very first act of therapeutic ethics, of absolute basics in communication (Grice, 1975), are bypassed, shallow framings invite mass identification, similar to horoscopes: each emotional state is rapidly named, diagnosed and 'solved', within seconds, as home remedy. As I clarified in an earlier work, this is not an accident but – as far as online content is concerned audience engagement is the most important aspect in content production, for staying relevant and helping the monetization engine. Furthermore, emotionally charged content works particularly well in engagement (Gross, 2024a). The structural incentive that rewards brevity and emotional stimulation over complexity, depth, ambiguity and sustained inquiry (which are the fundamental merits of clinical psychology and its approach to individual suffering) clearly oppose *genuine* healing.

It can be said that the spread of instant wisdom in the age of bite-sized information does not only trivialize psychological suffering but it also distorts it epistemologically. It replaces inquiry with proclamation and dialogue with prescription. Depth is bypassed to reach digestibility which translates into sales and reinforces a cultural atmosphere where suffering is no longer existential and relational, but as a problem for which there is an easy fix through surface level 'mental adjustments' (i.e., *mindset*), and this, by all means, is a betrayal of the very foundations of psychological understanding.

Up to this point, one may think that the accusations are quite obvious. But through deeper reflection, we may find that the core of the issue is much more systemic and grave, and reaches down to the very foundation of marketing and economic principle. In a world characterized by uncertainty – economic, societal, political, etc. – systemic precarity, fragmentation and volatility can take a heavy psychological and sociological toll. On this fertile ground, the promise of self-mastery and personal transformation has assumed an almost theological function. The psychological merits of this dynamic are not new; Aristotle recognized that within *pathos*

8

resides a potent driving force that compels individuals toward action: he acknowledged that harnessing people's fear and equally their hope are among the most powerful instruments in persuasion, as a part of rhetoric (Aristotle, 2007). He identified three modes of persuasion: ethos, pathos and logos. In the context of the self-help industry, pathos as the emotional appeal in the form of tapping into fear and hope can be seen as a powerful instrument to capitalize on individuals' innermost conflicts. The presentation of solutions that promise mastery and empowerment over one's circumstances aligns with Aristotle's understanding of how emotions are fallible and can be instrumentalized: while the promise of self-mastery can evoke hope, it serves as the counterbalance to the fear of failure and inadequacy.

Through this, the industry, or: *culture*, offers not merely advice for minor improvements; it presents a total narrative of deliverance, in recasting existential insecurity as a problem to be overcome through individual action. How handy it comes that the action plan is delivered right with that insight. However, this positioning reflects a deeper *psychopolitical* move (Han, 2017): the internalization of systemic chaos as personal inadequacy: rather than interrogating structural conditions responsible for widespread anxiety, self-help and mindset narratives displace the locus of suffering inward. The problem is not framed as belonging to the chaotic world, but to the individual who has failed to adapt, optimize and 'manifest' success. This includes the typical notorious '*American Dream*'-picturesque fallacy. You can achieve anything, and if you fail to achieve the best, you have not worked hard enough. Luckily, we can show you how. This is structural violence (Galtung, 1969), but alchemized into psychological defect. Collective reorganization or existential reflection are circumvented. The only demand is discipline, lived in instructed step by step selfreconstruction.

Not only is this marketable idea a myth, it also presumes omnipotent agency. Because in this framework, the individual is positioned as radically autonomous: capable of overcoming any obstacle, transcending any limitation, if only the right mindset, habit, technique is adopted. It would be too obvious to just conclude this is a selling feature. It goes beyond marketable strategy, it touches upon the existential. It is arrogance, it does not care about individual life stories, systemic limitations, inequalities, instabilities. All is irrelevant but the mindset and the will. Where there is a lack, it is the lack of will. Systemic denial in favor of a fantasy, of pure volition. Resilience becomes a moral imperative (we will encounter this word multiple times throughout this work). Vulnerability is shameful, particularly the kind that would demand collective response. Success is moralized, failure pathologized (Gill & Orgad, 2018).

Why is this narrative seductive? Again, because of the idea of agency. It offers coherence where reality does not. The inherent promise that meaning, control and security can be recovered through own, internal adjustments alone, sounds compelling. Systemic structures are absolved from critique and responsibility, because they are placed upon the individual – making instability intelligible and manageable through translating them into a personal project. This appeals to those seeking advice just as much as to those seeking existential relief. In the mind, a picture begins to form: of the individual that is expected to bear the full weight of structural disintegration without collective support or systemic change. This is the perfect loophole for a self-sustaining industry. In this very perpetuation, it ensures an experience of ongoing inadequacy with a continuous consulting for liberation.

The flourishing of the industry can not be understood in isolation from sociocultural transformations that have largely restructured the conditions of meaning-making. Traditional communal, spiritual and existential anchors have been progressively eroded in the modern, secularized and globalized world. A steady decline of social and cultural institutions that historically offered meaningful, existential frameworks and belonging has left the individual increasingly isolated, despite interconnectedness through electronic means. Where once existential uncertainty could be mediated through communal belonging, shared rituals and narratives, the modern human navigates their uncertainty largely alone. This emptiness is the vacuum where the self-help culture has placed itself with significant success, again negating all systemic circumstances, but therefore offering bite-sized, simplified and consumable answers to existential complexity. Life-hacks instead of metaphysical inquiry, affirmation instead of depth. Thus, the emergence of the self-help boom can be perceived and understood as structurally symptomatic, a direct response to atomization of meaning in late modernity.

Parallelly, labor as the economic substrate of life has undergone significant changes, and is still changing rapidly. The stability of long-term employment is just as much pathologized as predictable career trajectories – the *entrepreneurial self* is the new gold standard of labor, because herein lies a vast potential of further optimization. Unsurprisingly, everybody shall manage their own human capital and emotional labor, optimize their productivity, everyone is the CEO of their own life. Again, it also riddles down to the very individual who is no longer addressed as a member of a collective economic system, but rather as a singular agent with management capacity and responsibility, whose success or failure depends solely on their mindset, habits and so on. Systemic precarity as the perfect personal 'potential for development'. The prescription by the mindsetdoctors is simple: growth mindset, hustle mentality, overcoming challenges with the right techniques. In a market that never fails the individual, but rather the individual fails to adapt, the mindset culture becomes the maintenance system for precarious economy.

One understands that this structural uncertainty is not an accidental backdrop but rather the very precondition, fundamental to its core functionality. Fertile grounds of destabilized subjectivity nourish a narrative of reclaiming control, up to the point of invincible grandiosity. It makes the solutions a form of commodity, traded just where they are needed – psychic scaffolding. In reality, again, it is a system of self-sustenance: providing temporary relief, but deepening the dependency. Sold under the label of existential grounding, each bit subtly reinforces the premise that without continuing optimization, the self is doomed to stay defective, inadequate, alone.

At the heart of the act of self-optimization lies the paradox that the more one engages with all selfhelp advice, the more it often deepens confusion and fracture. This is not due to lack of motivation but to the overwhelming and often contradictory nature of the content itself. Each new principle seems to cancel the last, each new path implies a failure in the one previously taken, and the subject, rather than growing to resolution, becomes entrapped in a never-ending cycle, a carousel of shifting imperatives. It does of course not help that the diffuse nature and the endless range of choices contradicts itself permanently. Because every guru, every video, every book, every influencer, has *the* solution to the problem. The result is, psychologically, a loss of trust in one's inner compass. Inner reflection erodes further. Constant external validation of new methods, frameworks, mantras, can only disorient. Colloquially speaking: the more you try to 'fix' yourself, the more evidence you produce, that something is wrong. *With you.* This fragments the self instead of integrating it. While it could be argued that this might be an ironic side-effect, it should much rather be understood as a structural feature – a calm, content self does not generate demand. Instability is thus not a systemic bug, but the fuel that sustains the entire economy. Where every solution generates new friction, doubts and gaps to be filled, the next solution is already in the pipeline. The double logic is selling liberation while quietly maintaining dependence.

The premise is however unspoken: you are inadequate, hence you need to consume. This is transformation of suffering into a recurring subscription model where, in commercial terms, solutions are *intended* to be incomplete. While they shall be suggestive and motivating, may even feel temporarily relieving, they are always designed to leave room for more self-work, for nextlevel healing. The bar for success keeps moving with the subject. This is how anyone can morph into chronic inadequacy, since as each goal is approached, higher ones are introduced. A chronic, not-yet-complete self is cultivated.

Displacement of clinical models – conquering healing

The line between therapy and motivation has been srategically blurred. Clinical psychology, the domain of complexity, context and personal history, is a slow, relational and interpretive space. The self-help and mindset culture have repackaged it into streamlined motivation formulas. The subject is merely a productivity project in need of recalibration. Clinical models are attentive to ambivalence and unconscious conflicts, with resistance and contradiction, whereas the epistemic inversion of the 'motivational model' promises rapid results through motivational discourse, affirmation, action. Suffering is no longer to be understood, but just overcome. Management of inner life is preferred over exploration. Through that, depth is flattened ever more. The implications for the mind are further-reaching than it might seem at first glance, though. When motivational frameworks are marketed as substitutes for real psychological inquiry and work, individuals come to expect personal transformation as a product, that can be purchased, and without any discomfort. But herein lies the marketing lie: it is not possible to bypass existential suffering, confrontation and introspection. Healing is a practice and not a performance. It is not a spectacle of progress, just because the psychological is diminished to the behavioral.

Often, the narratives told are personal and appear to be a testimony of inner healing. Yet in many cases, they can be seen as a carefully curated entry point into a monetized system. Again lending from the *American Dream*-sort of storytelling, a journey from breakdown to breakthrough is deployed. Attention is immediately redirected toward the perfectly shining outcome. While the vulnerability shared is real enough to be engaging and relatable, suffering is a strategic hook that transitions into linear, repeatable and purchasable transformation – a profound distortion of what healing means. An interesting aspect is that the fragile and nonlinear nature of healing is not even counterintuitive to the subject. What is sold is simply the glossy-framed idea of bypassing the discomfort healing inherits. The healer / salesperson though, is granted authority to guide others not through knowledge, but through branding.

Apart from that, perhaps the most insidious maneuver in this curated economy is the redefinition of emotional suffering as 'latent capital'. Framed as unrealized potential for growth and aspiration, not as signals of unprocessed experience. Your suffering is a resource to be unlocked, we provide the key. This epistemological shift detaches suffering from its existential and psychological coordinates, as it neglects reflection, mourning, contextual analysis. It is all presented as evidence for untapped potential that can be capitalized through the right technique, the *alpha-mindset* or whatever else. This monetization of suffering undercuts an ethical gravity of magnitude. Psychic pain is nothing but a currency. It is recycled.

The problematic nature lies in the intolerance against all that is protected by depth psychology in a rigorous form: contradiction, ambivalence, a slow arc of integration. Operational scripts prohibit ontological richness and renders the entire reduction fully depersonalized. As a protocol of willpower, the individual is stripped of context, insight and richness. Moreover, complexity is punished. If you are anxious, you are thinking wrong. If you are poor, you manifest scarcity. If you feel lost, you need a stronger morning routine. Complexity and trauma mean wrong mindset. So why would these frameworks appeal to anyone? Firstly, because they are not directly and personally accused. In the one-size-fits-all approach lies anonymity, because it is exactly *not* a reflection. process between therapist and client, the salesperson does not know the subject it places its advicecorset onto. Secondly, it is the appeal of simplicity. The bypass. What lies beneath is misuse of psychological discourse and appropriation of language – profound epistemic falsification of what it means to suffer, to heal; to be human, ultimately. The ethical gravity lies in the loss of meaning of this discourse that swaps over into *real* psychological inquiry. Loss of grounding means psychological concepts become symbolic tokens, or pseudo-sacred words whose meanings shift based on market trend.

Emotional shallowness in binary vocabulary

Together with psychological language, human experience is also flattened and reduced. The complexity of emotional life is dissolved in hyper-articulated binary vocabulary of aligned or misaligned, good routine or bad routine, positive, negative, empowered or blocked. Emotional nuance is blurred out, where in clinical contexts, it is absolutely essential: sadness may comprise rage, joy may carry grief, despair can hold insight. But in the logic of the self-help marketplace, such ambiguity is a liability, it does not sell well. What sells is clarity, simplicity, action. 'High vibe' states are valorized, 'low frequency' is self-sabotage. All must fit into the corset of socially desirable – or not.

This conditions individuals into chronic self-monitoring for the purpose of creating ever-present space for self-improvement. Performance enhancement. Tracking habits, performance, routines, posture, mood, achievements – every facet of the self is a site for optimization, because it is *not enough to be*. One must be valuable. In marketable assets, that is. One must acknowledge and accept that they are a continuous project of reformation in response to external templates and metrics, that of course are designed to be unachievable, ultimately, which has disastrous implications. The chronic metric imposition fuels inner inadequacy more than ever, in real-time (Gross, 2024b). The perceived inadequacy of the self is profoundly fueled by subvert self-blame narrative, in the sense of a deeper sitting epistemic violence. Systemic issues – poverty, racism, structural injustice – are ignored. The problem is never the system, the problem is always *you*. This assumes the individual as fully sovereign and likewise offers the fantasy of ever-available success, if only one believes hard enough.

A paradox of manufactured suffering

At the heart of the self-help industry lies a structural paradox. The very system that promises psychological relief simultaneously reproduces and deepens the persistence of psychological disorientation that it depends upon. What presents itself as a healing culture is really a machinery that must sustain the experience of insufficiency in order to justify its very existence. This is not incidental or an unintended side-effect: the recurrence of failure and confusion, or temporary relief followed by deeper anxiety is of systemic design. The subject, once inducted into the self-help paradigm is no longer approached as a human being but as an optimization project. Logically, it must never be complete, as the lifeline of the industry is to always address the gap – the one that produces suffering.

The more one engages with the promises of empowerment and relief, the more the horizon of adequacy retreats. This works well, because the deeper the self-doubt, the more urgent the selfimprovement.

Psychologically, this amounts to an epistemic betrayal of healing. Wholeness is silently prohibited. Eva Illouz's (2007) critique of emotional capitalism verbalizes this logic in saying that therapeutic culture that is blended with market logics produces needs and anxieties in order to sell the claims of soothing them. It is exactly this dynamic that keeps the industry alive and well and extracts practically indefinite amounts of money from the burned-out modern life subject. This illuminates the exploitative nature of the field that keeps the individual from *being*.

Homo oeconomicus, the existential duty

The ideology behind the industry installs itself as a normative frame for self-understanding and transforms optimization from an optional pursuit into an existential imperative. The invitation becomes a moralized obligation to change, with subtle coercive elements. I call this logic *You can – therefore you must*. Freedom becomes mandate, contentment becomes guilt. This is a deeply ontological transition, because it entirely reorganizes agency, identity and worth. Existence itself is a failing product line in need of continuous updates.

Unsurprisingly, the psychological cost is immense: the individual begins to experience nonoptimization not as rest or reflection but a personal defect. Silence, stillness or uncertainty are reframed as laziness, weakness, stagnation. There is no space for existential integration. This cultural logic mirrors what Foucault (1980) thinks as a concept of disciplinary power that operates not primarily through force but through internalized norms. The individual is both the prisoner and guard in this panopticon, which extends to affect: emotions become the targets of regulation. In neoliberal logic, the individual is an entrepreneurial self, the homo *oeconomicus*, the dominant discourse must retrain the inner voice, not hear it. Hamann (2009), Yu (2023) and Filho et al. (2020) describe this process of self-monitoring and -assessment as a hybrid of freedom and obligation. The byproduct is a moralized affect: feeling bad equals being bad.

Demonization of contentment

The logic of the mindset-boom flips clinical psychology upside down. And that is, frankly, ridiculously shameless. Contentment and inner calmness are not celebrated as psychological health – they are pathologized. It is complacency.

Rest, satisfaction or the simple act of being are threats to growth and markers of mediocrity, insufficient ambition and of course, moral failure. One fails oneself if content. The subject is not invited to reflect their inner life, but rather urged to disrupt moments of stillness with the anxiety of missed potential. Serenity is not a socially desirable feature, it is unproductive. The forward momentum is the most important driver of sales, remember, thus the good life must be infinite trajectory. Fulfillment cannot logically exist in this realm, therefore any inner state of balance is 'premature'. Ahmed (2010) calls this the happiness injunction, which is a suitable term because it does not come from an innate desire but is externally fueled and incited. Furthermore, self-acceptance as a culturally sanctioned 'disobedience' with the narrative is enough to impose shame and blame.

In terms of clinical psychology, this forward momentum is at the expense of symbolic processing and concepts like regression, ambiguity and non-linearity. The soil of genuine transformation, this vectorial dimension of humanity is flattened to zero, because in the two dimensional world of the market, only growth matters. Integration is unmarketable.

But a culture that demonizes contentment can not allow healing.

Intellectual influences and traditions to situate this work

As a logic consequence of the above, this work is situated within a tradition of psychological inquiry that privileges and prioritizes depth, narrative and meaning over behavioral predictability or technical intervention. Its orientation is drawn not from any one school but from a constellation of thinkers and disciplines, closely observing the human psyche and the existential dilemmas of modernity.

From the domain of psychodynamic theory, this work takes the stance that symptoms are not surface-level malfunctions but encrypted messages, as signs of unresolved inner conflicts and repressed meaning. Suffering can be comprised of much, but should be perceived as failure of translation between enigmatic messages and the human inner world. This shall remind us that the psyche is never transparent to itself and the work of understanding can never be reduced to technique; symptom formation is not a human deficit but a narrative event to be listened to.

From an existential foundation, the ontological vertigo of freedom, the burden of choice and the inevitability of human despair while longing for meaning owe to thinkers like Kierkegaard, Sartre and Camus. In an indifferent or even absurd kind of world, this work borrows notions from existential psychology and philosophy, that remind us that suffering is not a flaw to be erased but a condition of becoming human.

Synthesizing existentialists and psychodynamic inquiry with critical standpoints, and -tradition, this work brings about the interrogation of the sociocultural circulation of emotion and psychological discourse. In this analysis, self-help and mindset cultures are understood as elements of soft control.

Through these lenses, this work is an invitation to reclaim depth and return to the roots of psychological reflection, where the human condition is treated with dignity. In this sense, it is not a critique from the outside but rather a reclamation from within the psychological discipline which has seen its depth hollowed out for long enough by modern culture. At its core, this is meant as a deliberate confrontation with the cultural grammars that shape modern discourse and it firmly positions itself against the logic that every crack in the human soul is a business opportunity. It consciously refuses to reproduce the format of intervention and instead offers a manifest honoring pain in recognition of disorientation. It does not persuade, though. It invites.

Healing, if it is to deserve the name, must begin with truthful understanding. Thus, the following reflection is grounded in the conviction that psychological life needs psychological integrity. In an era where the mind is under siege by metrics, slogans and affective manipulation, such protection begins with critique.

Part I

Epistemic Reconfiguration – How Psychology is Hollowed Out

1 THE INDUSTRY OF SUFFERING: FROM CLINICAL INQUIRY TO COMMODITY

1.1 Emotional Capitalism: Psychological Struggle as Marketable Resource

In the historical grammar of psychology, emotions have always signified rupture. They emerged as expressions of deeper conflict, symptoms of repression, or signals of unmet needs. In psychoanalytic thought, the symptom was meaningful precisely because it resisted immediacy – it demanded interpretation as opposed to extraction. Emotion, in this context, is interpreted as an inner contradiction slowly surfacing into consciousness: as a sign that something in the inside does not cohere. This incoherence requires the slow and, at times, solemn labor of integration (Freud, 1917/1957; Laplanche & Pontalis, 1973). Within the framework of therapeutic inquiry, emotion is an entry point into depth and intuitive interpretation. It has nothing to do with market linguistics.

But this solemnity is at stake.

In the affective economy of mindset-, self-help, and influencer culture, emotions are being recoded: not as existential disturbances but rather as marketable assets. Feelings are units of a currency that drives engagement, generates visibility and accrues value through publicity. The interiority of emotional life is becoming an opportunity space; branding, monetization, narrative capital. Sadness, vulnerabilities and even trauma are no longer withheld or explored slowly and respectfully, but are immediately reprocessed into stylized disclosure. The demand is for revelation, not reflection. And this revelation is best when it performs in one way or another.

But this shift is not only a cultural transformation, it can rather be described as an epistemic mutation. The interpretive pause that once followed surfacing emotion is no longer adequate in this new paradigm, it is rather a demand for instantaneous instrumentalization. Instead of exploring what *a feeling means*, the question is now *how it can be used*. Emotional expression, consequently, is no longer embedded in a therapeutic temporality but a digital one. Illouz (2007) uses this exact development as her case model for explaining *emotional capitalism*, in emotions being made assets, commodifying affect to replace ambiguous inner life. What you feel, as a consequence, matters only to the extent that it can be packaged, or converted, into insight, a *lesson*, a growth narrative, an aesthetic breakdown. This is production replacing protection.

This makes emotions 'social technologies' (Ahmed, 2014) that bind the subject not only to people but to ideological formations, in the sense of what can be leveraged from feelings and inner conflict. Everything functions as a call to action in this culture. An activation point. A pivot for your life, ground for transformation to better alignment with what should be. Mourning is obsolete. It is static, it does not drive momentum.

This leads to the narrowing of space, there is no longer any reflective room for ambivalence of life, and for the idea that feelings might not be immediately *useful*. Feelings might simply *be*; they are signs of a life lived in tension, in conflict, and not in control. The hollowing of emotional complexity is disguised as empowerment, that everyone should be pursuing. The real performance though, is displacement of inner truth, for the sake of external yield. When you are prompted to convert, not invited to feel, the very feelings that once pointed to inner truth are now a tool, mobilized to sell to you the fantasy of resolution.

But the contemporary self-help economy performs a more sophisticated move than just instrumentalizing emotion: it turns suffering into *content*, it transforms it into a narrative product. What was once a signal of psychic rupture and invited therapeutic witnessing or symbolic integration, is now framed and crafted for consumption. Pain is formatted. Exploration is too timeconsuming and does not yield an 'outcome' worth pursuing. Nowhere is this better visible than in the influencer ecosystem, where platforms reward disclosure that adheres to a particular grammar of redemption. The logic behind this is clear: a crisis is only worth sharing if it arrives with closure, insight and aesthetic. One can not hurt unless it is *growth*, and public. Algorithmic proof of one's journey, a curated montage of healing as content.

This nudges the subject to reverse-engineer their pain: translate it to the language of breakthrough, empowerment, 'radical authenticity', just not authentic. Vulnerability can be used in a strategic way, as long as suffering is a brand asset. Every breakdown, if well-narrated, can be made attractive and secure further engagement, follower loyalty. Messages shall be clear, not the sometimes enigmatic depth of psychic life. That does not sell well. This mines the inner world, instead of accompanying it. The attention economy has no usability for a confidential emotional container, so if something is not a task, is not published and resolved, who would want that. Pain, however, does not adjust to that narrative, because it is simply not how it works. The inner existential protest stays, the symbolic interruption stays, however much it may be distorted. Because this is not what suffering is. Suffering is not a product.

Therefore, however much influencer discourse tries to present this as empowerment, the subject can not make their pain meaningful in real time. As Abidin (2016) and Garde-Hansen & Gorton (2013) note, parasocial connections in influencer culture create the illusion of intimacy while actually hollowing out the space for genuine psychological process: this makes the follower emulate, but not reflect their inner world. With emotional inarticulacy, but with aesthetic appeal. The pain that does *not* resolve? Inefficient. Realities, but inadmissible. In the disembodied model of the narrative economy, this does not belong.

The symptom, once the cornerstone of psychological inquiry, is no longer treated as symbolic conflict. Clarity is the new paradigm, and in the fundamental displacement of the clinical dimension by the consumable, a symptom is, before all, a content opportunity. The self-help marketplace does not ask what it is trying to say, but rather what the audience wants to hear. Therapeutic encounter, driven and defined by curiosity, humility and ambiguity, is too hesitant for the instant clarity that delivers performance. Here, the consumer is both patient and market – and the role of the clinician is not assumed by a trained observer but by a performer who delivers insight. Aesthetic containers like reels, posts, courses, offered by mindset coaches and influencers repackage psychological language. However, their power does not lie in listening, but in claiming authority over what struggle means. The more shareable, repeatable and frictionless, the better. Accuracy is not necessary because there is no relation and no accountability. Illouz (2008) lays out a seminal cultural diagnosis here: where therapy becomes persuasion, the clinician becomes the seller of clarity.

The consequence is more than just dilution. It is substitution – epistemic. Immediate knowability defies the logic of clinical psychology, that requires sitting with contradiction and delay. But that can not be consumed, it can not be *made* consumable. Complexity is a liability that such a market can not afford, because the depth of it is inefficient. This fundamental distortion has severe consequences for how people now approach their own experience. The go-to is now self-work via protocols, course programs, subscription-based self-assessment. Healing is a solo-project, happening by the side line. It can be upon narrative coherence, and its structure and linearity at all times. Providers of clarification do not need to listen, it is irrelevant because they can provide solutions without even knowing the problem. Now if that is not efficient. How frustrating ambiguity is. Who needs co-interpretation of psychic material anyway. Pain is a serviceable mood that can be redirected into empowerment. As Foucault (1980) suggested, the domain of what is considered intelligible is never neutral; it is constructed through regimes of power and discourse. Accordingly, the depth of the subject is simply ignored into irrelevance.

1.2 The Appropriation of Psychological Language in Influencer Ecosystems

Foundational psychological concepts like trauma, attachment and anxiety have lost their clinical specificity in modern environments of self-help and social media. They have been transformed and morphed into stylistic signatures. These terms now function less as diagnostic or interpretive categories and more as mere branding tools. While they signal a kind of cultural literacy, they display an insider status within the therapeutic vernacular. Speaking of one's 'attachment style' or posting about 'anxiety issues' is no longer a genuine engagement with inner life, but rather a claim of fluency in the dominant language of emotional culture.

Identity signifiers – tools for aesthetic positioning in digital economies, what were once frameworks for inquiry in depth and humility, of relational understanding. Creators outline the signs of anxiouspreoccupied attachment with fancy music and a personal narrative, probably even made up in its entirety, reducing a multi-layered relational history into a 60-second emotional typology. Instead of clinical depth, *relatability* is the be all and end all, because it means engagement, resonance, reach. Through this, psychological terms have become semiotic capital – circulating for connection, for their appeal of familiarity, viral malleability. Popular psychological discourse increasingly popularizes and hypes immediacy and recognizability. This can only come at the expense of nuance and understanding. In particular, emotionally stimulating and charged content is predestined for virality, as I have explained in a previous work (Gross, 2024a). In this regard, trauma is not a structural impact, but a tone. Attachment is a dating app filter. Anxiety is not representative of inner conflict, but a hashtag with billions of views.

Unfortunately, this transformation does not only hollow out meaning. And nor does the danger lie in trivialization. Rather, the purpose of psychological language gets confused altogether, the terms *invert*. They provide the illusion of self-knowledge and inhibit the labor of self-understanding, make self-discovery obsolete. Declaring one's 'trauma' explains away all further need for interpretation. This is semantic comfort, without existential contact.

This can be understood as the construction of split digital personae – I have extensively examined that concept in previous works (Gross, 2024b). There is not the suffering individual; there is the individual signaling their suffering as a feature of their public identity. Illuoz (2008) notes that therapeutic language has long since escaped the clinic. But now, we are witnessing a conversion of that language into personal capital, to be shared, monetized, to yield performance. Anxiety and trauma are recycled for content, theory and depth is simplified into scripts. Psychological complexity is dissolved into 'emotional style'.

Therapy has acquired an aesthetic grammar of its own in the visual, pastel-tone self-help economy. It must be emotionally performative, and healing is not something that someone undergoes, and endures, but that it shown. It needs performative character. The therapist is a public figure, not a companion to suffering, they are framed by soft lighting and captioned insights. The patient is not shielded by confidentiality and the unspoken but becomes a content creator of their own, uploading pain in digestible formats. This is not to be understood as a critique of media per se, but of what happens when therapeutic engagement is translated into visual style. The temporality of healing slow, recursive – is ill-suited to the temporal logic of public social media platforms. Immediacy, repetition and emotional grab are simply not the right seedbed for the transformative character of psychic inquiry and understanding. The symbolic labor of therapeutic work is now what Baudrillard (1994) might call a simulation: an image of therapy that replaces therapy itself. The slide carousel explaining 'trauma bonding in five steps' and calming ASMR voice reciting 'you are safe', 'you are enough' are not holding, are not therapy – but they circulate as though they were.

All these mantras in serif font over desaturated background, motivational memes, instand wisdom insights are designed not to provoke thought but to reassure the warm feeling of familiarity. This is why it works so well. Relatable slogans in a therapeutic aesthetic signal intimacy, but provide pseudo-relation. They bypass actual presence.

Digital wellness content often mimics the tone of therapeutic presence while offering none of its ethical or relational substance. And that, precisely, is the problem.

In this context, the aspects that are central to clinical psychological work – contradiction, silence, resistance – are excluded in this discourse. Affective clarity is in demand and therethrough, the content frame gives clear instructions of what healing must or must not consist of, of what aesthetic coherence the self can be comprised, and of what it may not. This presents to the individual how they should feel, look and heal. This, logically, encourages a performance of healing in a certain structure, but not clinically grounded. For reassurance, one can always consult back to the overarching authorities governing the discourse: 'Does this look like trauma?'; and 'Does this look like healing?'.

This primary mode of emotional identification is a gateway into consumer capture, not a clinical step forward. Just watch the right video or subscribe to the right course, choose your diagnosis in one click. ADHD or rejection sensitivity? Anxious attachment or depression, OCD, Borderline personality disorder? You might also be interested in how to recognize a narcissist by 3 bulletproof telltale signs. These are not clinical hypotheses, these are marketing hooks. They are keywords that are affectively resonant and initiate the user into a narrative of personal brokenness, but don't worry, they're of course followed by a sequence of purchasable solutions. Link in the description.

This conversion logic is not at all incidental – the relatability in the discourse makes for a streamlined process of relating to a syndrome, framed with glitter and compassion, clicking to 'learn more', resonating with the provided content. Thereby, diagnosis is a marketing funnel that directs the individual to the next offer: a workshop, a course, a subscription service. What has been vague unease, an internal struggle, is now behavioral branding as a product-aligned self-conception. The '*Hey, that's me*'-effect. Algorithmic influence, of course, becomes the primary tool. Modern algorithms reinforce this process because the more one relates with the content, the more one receives. Platforms reward prolonged engagement and emotional reactivity (Gross, 2024a). Thus, what we can see is *diagnostic affinity*. As Crary (2013) argues in a different context, there is a market value in the neoliberal subject, that is best carved if they are awake, anxious and consuming. Never at rest because their malaise is endlessly prolonged but never resolved. The endless agitation is the most valuable soil for monetary exploitation because restlessness prompts action. A fundamental 'insight': it works for finance, it works for psychological unease.

The fundamental problem is the individual's understanding. It is a short-circuit where the emotional experience is narrowed to pre-scripted symptomatology, in that the subject no longer explores what is unique, biographic or difficult in their suffering, but rather searches for matches. The label offers relief, but not in the sense of therapeutic insight. It is well documented that diagnoses give language to inner distress and thus lead to recognition, validation and relatability (Huibers & Wessely, 2006; Parker, 2010; Rosenfield, 1997), and eventually they provide access to treatment – which is the logic that the self-help and mindset industry have successfully 'hacked'. This identity becomes comforting, but also functions as a confinement. Conveniently, it places the consumer in a readymade preset vertical of tailored solutions. We've got just the right thing for *people like you*. You are not only struggling, but you are struggling like someone with X, and X has a program.

This is decontextualization of clinical language, as a product interface. Rose (1999) warned a long time ago that the privatization of psychological knowledge under neoliberalism erodes not only the content of this knowledge but also the ethical foundations. And boy, was he right. When diagnosis becomes content, and content is commerce, then there's only one question left to be answered: 'What must I buy for deliverance?'.

1.3 Bypassing Therapeutic Dialogue: Prescription Without Presence

Therapeutic discourse ought not to give answers but allow for encounter. The space of therapy in its clinical integrity is not organized around content but relation. Slow and dialogical. It unfolds where the individual is not treated as a problem to be solved but as a psyche to be heard. It comprises intersubjective depth and mutual presence – and that, precisely, makes it distinct from instruction and advice. Wampold (2015) beautifully brings to attention the fact that the therapeutic encounter, together with the common factors, drive therapeutic value and change. Solutionist, script-based formats are the exact opposite. It is not a one-directional relationship. It is not protocol. The knowledge about the importance of alliance in psychology is not new but is simply ignored and overwritten in this *simulation* of support. Coaching culture, responsive in tone, performatively empathic, is still structurally absent. In context and in encounter.

What is not consumed in place of therapy is a rotating archive of answers. We offer everything from blueprinted bullet point solutions, neatly packaged mantras, short-form videos to go. The influencer as guru speaks in clear formulations, the reel-structure is nice and familiar. Thankfully, the script provides the sequence of this transaction, so the speaker does not need to know the listener.

In this narrative choreography, there is a rhythm of empathy, but it does never risk intimacy. How convenient, because it is scalable and also technologically accelerated. Though the phenomenon is not new. Again, mid-20th century, Carl Rogers claimed unconditional (positive) regard and empathic understanding, not as techniques but as *stances* in ways of being with a person to foster growth and healing. It is the clear opposite of 'Here's what to do next' (cf. Rogers, 1957). The psychological absence becomes cumulative when every wound is met with a sequential solution. It translates the subject's complexity into inefficiency. The lack of presence manages the individual, instead of guiding them. While the own voice becomes inconvenient, healing transforms into compliance with the externally imposed script.

Imagine this as being handed coordinates that show the bypass of pain, which needs no company. Promising clarity, the reality is a disconnection. The scripts do not fail because of their simplicity, but because they have no relational character, by design: they answer what has never been asked, and respond where no self has ever spoken.

What gives words their weight is their relation, the attunement and resonance. They are not hollow phrases without history and depth. But here, in the self-help and coaching culture's dimensions, they are disembodied, instruction, transaction. In this landscape, the subject's life has no chronology, no unconscious structure and no story. The guru does not know what came before and they don't want to know. Because all that matters is the urgency of the present, the present 'mindset', the step to take. Advice floats, untethered, indifferent to the life in which it is being inserted.

To address someone without knowing where they have been is to speak not to them but over them.

The relational field, the attunement, affective presence, mutual implication, are the core of psychodynamic understanding (Ogden, 1994; Wachtel, 2008) that is erased here. It is replaced with a hollow form of pseudo-empathy that only mimics care, but only on the surface; it is stripped of all history.

There is, of course, a predictable defense against this critique. The self-help industry does not present itself as therapeutic encounter, but as careful architectural support. Its spokespeople claim not to be analysts or companions, but facilitators – "enablers," "empowerers," designers of frameworks through which individuals can heal themselves. In this telling, the absence of attunement is not a flaw, but a feature. Of course there is no resonance, no presence – and none is promised. The guru, after all, is merely offering tools. It is the individual who does the work. This rationale is compelling because it draws upon the dominant moral grammar of autonomy and selfdetermination. Who, after all, knows you better than you? So there – by this logic – is the attunement. There is the relation. You speak, and you listen. To yourself. But what appears humble and self-effacing is in fact a philosophical sleight of hand. And it is a dangerous one.

Because in psychoanalytic terms, you cannot be the subject *and* the analytic third. You cannot simultaneously speak from within your psychic reality and listen to it from elsewhere. The analytic third, as Ogden (1994) articulates, is not a role but a field – a relational space that emerges between two people, charged with difference, tension, rupture, and recognition. It is not introspection. It is intersubjectivity. It is not simply the act of telling, but of being heard in a way that alters the very meaning of what is told.

The predictable counter-argument is the carefully staged pseudo-humility of the self-help voice: it does not simulate intimacy, it insists – it only equips. But what it proposes instead is the emulation of an analytic third within the self – as if one could generate therapeutic resonance in solitude, without the presence of another. The appeal is clear: between oneself and oneself, there is obviously no friction. But this is not how meaning is made.

McAdams (1993) reminds us that identity is not a monologue but a co-authored narrative – the story of the self is developed, tested, and transformed in relation. One cannot encounter the full weight of suffering without another to receive it, to reflect it back, to disturb its circularity. Attempting to narrate oneself in isolation may produce the form of self-understanding, but not its substance. It reinforces what already is, rather than opening what might be. Self-help may offer the grammar of psychological narration, but not the *dialogical field* in which narration becomes transformative.

And this failure is not neutral. It is not like adding water to water. It is like adding acid. Because it quietly reinforces the original wound: to be unseen, misunderstood and bypassed. The advice may be well-meaning, the tone may be gentle, but the structure itself is alienating for the subject is still fundamentally alone in their struggle. It recapitulates abandonment, offers direction without presence, speech without listening, language without relationship. And in doing so, it deepens alienation.

This entire epistemic shift makes healing a procedure by protocol. Abstract inner life is sliced into solvable units, where emotion, trauma, identity are governed by applicable rules. They are to be learned and applied and with the right action steps, the algorithm of expected outcomes is also predictable. But even though the self-help industry thrives on this very reduction, it is fundamentally incompatible with how human change actually occurs. Buber (1937/2000) distinguishes between an I-*it* and an I-*thou* relation, where healing happens only in the latter. The presence of the other ('thou') is necessary because it holds. The relation can not be a tool or a function, there must be a space between two selves. Substituting this encounter is simply not possible because psychological space for transformation is not mechanical, it is lived. An individual does not heal because they have successfully accomplished the 'five steps to childhood integration' (link in the description), they heal when they are seen. When the unspeakable is spoken – and held.

In this compliance over complexity logic, healing is measured by the reduction of symptoms. Or, the reduction of symptoms, per time. Because pain must pass – and efficiently. This is finest 'therapy culture' as it is understood by Furedi (2004) who laid out the cultural context of how therapy is normalized as emotional management. One that conforms with new cultural-emotional norms instead of responding to suffering. And all of that amounts to another deep epistemic betrayal: the procedural sale of healing is not a clinical misunderstanding but a denial of the very condition that makes healing possible – relationship.

1.4 From Symptom to Slogan

Interpretation has been replaced in the economy of emotional content. Psychological aphorisms issue closure, they do not invite reflection. Instead of opening meaning, it is sealed. Despite circulating as therapeutic utterances, they perform epistemic foreclosure: complexity and individuality of emotional life is evacuated and in its place emerges the slogan: short and assertive. *Non-negotiable.*

Statements like 'you are enough' are not false. The reason why they are problematic is rather that they are issued as indiscussable. They can not be unpacked, or questioned, or complicated. They stand. Just like that. Questioning or interpretively complicating them is to violate the emotional norms they enforce. Through that, they install an injunction under the guise of comfort: the listener can not respond 'But I don't feel enough'. There is simply no space for contradiction, ambiguity or individual ambivalence. Through that, slogans in pseudo-psychological discourse are, again, deeply violent, for they obliterate meaning-making and instead command to agree. This offers no dialogical pathway. It simulates care, but exploration is not permitted. Wittgenstein (1953) warned that language can both relieve and imprison, and these slogans rather function as prescriptive speech acts (cf. Searle, 1975). Wittgenstein's (1953) insights lead us to the judgment that language gains meaning through its use in specific contexts – as opposed to being a static essence. If they are abstracted from relational and dialogical function, they perform no social and reflective work. Based on this principle, we observe that rather than being open-ended reflections – to engage, inquire, negotiate – they are aphorisms used to foreclose. They cease to operate in what Wittgenstein calls a *language-game*: they command, and instruct a feeling and closes the door behind the instruction, rather than holding space for the feeling. This is a grammatical illusion.

The therapeutic register, however, tolerates the unsaid. Therapeutic language allows hesitation and misalignment. It is *not* sealed. It is not a circular logic. And above all, it is not assaulting. Whereas, in pop discourse, expressing discomfort with 'good vibes only' is equal to bringing negativity into the space. That's the unspeakable things. That's not acceptable inner life. This is exactly the form of 'cruel optimism' in affective capitalism that Berlant (2011) describes: the epistemic violence of motivational aphorisms, that, while promising salvation, do not help the subject think but help the system remain unthought.

If complexity becomes unspeakable, then reflection without a definitive and unambiguous conclusion is no longer intelligible. One can not any longer remain in any form of psychological tension without thinking wrongly. Unresolved insights, painful contradiction, *the fabric of living*, is punishable. They are errors in communication, wrong thinking, failures in attitude. The unequivocal demand for brevity has conquered the therapeutic terrain of unfinished emotional truth: unless contained in a readily available solution, complexity is not permitted to exist in public speech. Through that, psychological subjectivity itself is actively negated. Therein lies a poisonous logic, if observed closely: the psyche, by nature a field of disorder – fragmented, emergent, contradictorily layered – is treated as *defective*. The motion of the psyche is between registers, it is knowing and not-knowing, revealing and withholding, speaking and silencing and that is the substance of therapeutic encounter (Bollas, 1987; Laub, 1992) – however, that defect is to be managed. It violates the pace of motivation.

Bourdieu (1991) argues that what is speakable is real. In experience, that is. Coming from that logic, your feelings are no longer valid if they are unspeakable. A governed discourse of what is legitimate to be felt and to identify with governs the validity of the emotion as well. Your complexity is noise, and it should slowly cease to exist. The system narrows language to what is acceptable and erases from the speech-space what can not be consumed and sold. And again, we face the binary nature in discourse, where the subject is not granted a process but only a position. Growing or stagnant. Your story is empowering or negative. Aligned or blocked.

What appears as a linguistic discussion at surface level is, in my opinion, a deep disintegration of psychological experience, and of violent magnitude: to feel something but to lack the format to say it. Your inner life, unshared – and unsharable.

The final stage of language collapse within the self-help and mindest economy is that language no longer mediates between the subject and the experience. It completely bypasses subjectivity and treats emotional life as a site for real-time regulation. 'Let go of what no longer serves you' does never seek context. 'Focus on the positive (or: the small) things in life' does not *care* what is also true. They are affective orders and reduce the complexity of inner life and human experience to descriptive directives about how one should feel. There is no more function of symbol, let alone elaboration. It is mood governance (Rimke, 2000). A vehicle for correction. Instead of asking questions and getting into meaningful dialogue, one

gets an imperative. And yet again, there is potential to optimize. Behavioral scripting in motivational syntax. The insidious feature behind it is the simulation of psychological care.
While it delivers the opposite of holding, that is. Rose (1999)
identified this dynamic in his analyses of the psychological
subject under neoliberalism: a shift from dialogue to alignment; a demand for the compliance with the correct emotional
protocol. This is hideous. Because is devoids psychological
speech of content and meaning while still preserving its ap-
pearance. How is the subject to differ, if words like 'healing',
'trauma', 'authenticity', 'attachment', 'self-awareness' are re-
tooled to serve self-management, in the sense of motivational
mantras and hollow narrative?

2 ALGORITHMIC AFFECT: THE DIGITAL CIRCULATION OF EMOTIONAL LIFE

2.1 Emotional Expressions as Engagement Currency

Digital culture has established itself as the source of almost all information, entertainment and everything in between. So it comes that emotional disclosure no longer operates in the domain of intimacy but is broadcasted as just another act of performance, and one that is governed by algorithmic logic. As opposed to personal necessity, that is. This expression happens in an anticipation of response, and that response is not by a relational other but rather an abstract statistic. An algorithmic audience. As Winnicott (1965) explains, disclosing an emotional truth is to enter a space of admitting oneself to risk: a vulnerability, non-instrumental, that demands containment. The predictable beat of raw confession, followed by a pivot of insight and a prompt for others to 'relate' is quite the opposite. And it is not true, either. A holding environment that allows to feel into oneself and to speak difficult truths brings someone's inner world into a shared reality. And that is a risk because it is not shouting into a void, it is a truth held by a presence, with reflection (Winnicott, 1965). In the closed loop of digital architecture, curation is what discerns the true from the false self (Gross, 2024b). The algorithm, the heartbeat of the modern internet culture, dictates the pace and form of content and the aesthetics of digital self-representation are no exception. And in that, visibility is the new container for pain.

As Goffman (1959) observed long before the digital age, all self-presentation contains a certain aspect of performance – but in today's landscape, this performance is *total*. His insights comprise the presentation of self and the respective domains where it happens; *front stage*, the realm of public interaction where social scripts are the frame for behavior and act. But *backstage*, where the mask slips, where decompression happens and contradicting truths emerge, is the counterpart. The tension between these two spaces is where the self is; the dichotomy between social mask and inner life. In that, performance is not inherently inauthentic. But this was long before the digital age.

Where Goffman identified that we are never entirely *false*, nor *real*, the tension between the two worlds, the ethical ambiguity of this membrane, there is nowadays a screen, algorithmic governance and performance without any belief. There is no backstage. There is only the stage and anonymity, content aesthetic against a void. This phenomenon is laid out in contemporary literature, explaining that emotional truth has become a tool for the maintenance of the online relevance: emotional disclosure is subject to engagement metrics like comments, likes, shares and instead of personal catharsis is serves for the sustenance of one's presence and engagement in the ever-evolving digital sphere (Dobson, 2015).

What we can see here is the opposite of Goffman's logic: there is no longer person and persona – all melts into one. Through that, algorithmic mechanisms rewire emotional literacy: they shape its form and its affective arc. Grief is rewarded, but only so long it follows a redemption. It may well feel like failure until it can be flipped into being *productive*. The algorithm is the new digital superego.

2.2 The Platform Logic of Healing

From what has been established, it can be argued that healing is no longer a process in algorithmic platform dynamics. On digital terrain, the logic of shareability is dogmatic and never debated. As the algorithm acts as an invisible filter that quietly removes what is too slow, too ambiguous or context-specific, it is the absolute authority over discourse. However, the consequences reach far beyond the 'feed'. Where virality and visibility eclipse validity, this absolutist filtering mechanism not only applies to external recognition. It begins to shape the very way the subject listens inward. Attention is not only redirected by others, but by the self. In essence, the question of what gets seen becomes gradually indistinguishable from what is felt.

Algorithms are essentially reinforcement systems. But they do not only *learn* from reinforcement, they also reinforce; it is the user who is most profoundly trained (Gross, 2024a). This makes them functionally and psychologically reinforcing – over time, the logic of affective reward, in the shape of views, likes, affirmation, rewires the subject's internal attention economy toward a privilege for only those kind of feelings that match the recognizable high-yield categories ('growth', 'breakthrough', 'resilience',...). And this, frankly, is not only mimicry – it is affective restructuring of consciousness. In clinical terms, it amounts to psychic injury. Repetition installs architecture: the longer and more frequently the subject is exposed to and confronted with algorithm-mediated feedback loops, the more they adopt and internalize the framework of affective relevance into their own self-perception. What began as a public filter is becoming an internalized one.

Gillespie (2018) describes how platform infrastructures actively rank content according to affective rhythms that most likely generate high engagement. While this structural logic is widely known nowadays, it is rarely acknowledged that it translates to a sorting principle of the inner world just as well:

a silent, gradual curation of one's own emotions, in alignment with the governance of machine-determined discourse.

Is this a rhetorical exaggeration? I think it is a foundational epistemic corruption of inner listening. Classical clinical theory – particularly in relational and object-relations traditions – has long emphasized that affective experience emerges in the space of encounter, and gains coherence through the reflective process with an analytic third who contains (cf. Winnicott, 1965; Stolorow et al., 1994). Constant inward monitoring in anticipation is certainly not what clinical theory means. Worse even, this is no longer just for the persona; as already established, person and persona become indistinct from one another in this economy. There is no more unformatted and protected self beneath the surface. The surveillance has become structural. Inner life is sorted by predicted compatibility with algorithm demands, and what can not be harvested can become unfelt. Because the self-help economy stands at the opposite side of emotional epistemology: no language, no frame, no holding space.

There is no counterbalance for the individual. No external referent, no clinical authority that would allow individuals to challenge this profoundly distorted logic of inner listening. There is just the deus ex machina of modern suffering that has colonized the entire perceptual field.

2.3 The Metrics of the Self: Quantification and Self-Understanding

The rise of mood apps, journaling systems and dashboards of all kinds has ushered in a new ontology of selfhood, one that is rooted in data instead of intuition. The self is now a behavioral sequence that can be charted, measured and improved. And improvement must be visible, it is no longer *subjective* or felt, improvement can nowadays only be expressed in comparable numbers. The subjectivity that once defined what the self is has transformed into a spreadsheet whose sum is the individual. This model sure has its seductive character for a reason: clarity, among all features, is the most sought after in such an ambiguous and often counterintuitive and confusing world and life. It comes in handy that graphs and trendlines seem to provide a non-negotiable overview of how it looks in oneself and where the weak spots are. After all, a chain is only as strong as its weakest link, is it not?

The subtle reconfiguration of psychic experience into logs of character, mood and habit can help you determine where the right intervention must take place. Recurrence can be calculated, productivity can be tracked and anticipated. Data obsession is not unique to mind sciences, though.

However, at the center of the new self is the concept of gamification. The inflation of token economy. Badges, streaks, all sorts of behavioral incentives are used to structure self-regulation these days. Behavioral economics and Skinnerian conditioning let self-care perform (Schüll, 2016). Have you been grateful today? Tick the box. Have you told yourself the mantra about being enough? Hydrated? Your breathing points are on their way. And that is your new relationship to yourself?

Lupton (2016) notes how this 'data doublehood' splits the self into the lived experience and its digital representation. It is a complete reconstruction on the screen, but one in which subjective experience is overwritten for the interface. That is because the digital self becomes dominant rapidly. I am not only concluding wildly: imagine the progress you are trying to make and that the lived experience is no longer valid in and of itself. The game whose rules are invisible but whose scoreboard you can track is now also the representation of your inner life. And what happens if the scoreboard shows no improvement? Then your lived perception is no longer epistemically valid. The app has become an authority. Why would an industry want to do that, one might ask.

Because it is a means of careful preparation. It prepares the consumer for the next solution. A plateau in data is no problem, do not worry. New products are already in the pipeline and they have just what you need; new opportunities to intervene and better in every possible fashion. New mood apps with more granular sleep tracking. The better calibrated data can finally reveal your true inner conflict and why it was self-evident that your previous routines and attempts failed. Selfoptimization becomes a cult of self-consumption, and self-care is to tell yourself to analyze your dashboard. The solution is just a purchase away. This is not already a premature conclusion of what the next thought axis will be – the systematic manufacture and maintenance of suffering. But it can be seen as paving the way there, an overture. The architecture slowly peels itself: an infrastructure needed to commodify incremental dissatisfaction. You log not how you feel, but how much better you could be. With the right tools at hand, that is.

The technical illusion of insight because of 'datafication' seems to offer control over what was previously unruly. Levay et al. (2020) recognize the appeal that quantification has and call numbers productive *as well as deceptive and seductive* – in that they offer communicative acts of measurement but they can also have unintended effects because they take an aura of authority. Quantification, in essence, produces a sense of depth that is not always true. Especially for the human being, quantification removes layers of depth that can not be expressed in numerical data which is pretty much the essence of *the* discussion going on in modern psychology. White (2017) describes how, among other aspects of life, the qualitative nuance is ignored in favor of numbers, the very non-utilitarian aspects that make the individual unique and valuable. But humans are ultimately easily deceived by authoritative appeal. And that is what numbers do: most people simply do not understand them and trust in the 'magic' that they do. The science-aesthetic and apparent superiority of quantifiable data become the new proxy for judgment simply because of their appeal – and, of course, of their convenience.

2.4   Fragmentation, Over-Choice and Contradictory Frameworks

As a natural byproduct of a market as hopelessly flooded as the self-help and mindset economy, contradiction is inevitable. The sheer volume of competing advice, gurus, coaches, books, and influencers does quite the opposite of clarifying anything for the individual. Of course each of the outlets for themselves promises the path to illumination. But what compass would one trust?

In this regard, one of Erikson's (1959) most critical insights is that the ego, as the self's central organizing unit, has a deeply integrative function. It does not mean to eliminate conflict to resolve it. Rather, containment and synthesis of internal tensions do stabilize human experience into a sense of self, across time and context. Responsibility and desire, past and future, dependence and autonomy. A healthy ego is one that can bear contradiction without immediate collapse, it is the meaning of psychological strength, or: resilience, and a coherent narrative. Experiencing oneself as whole, across and despite contradiction and ambiguity is what makes identity non-static, but a dynamic achievement from experiences. The self-authored life narrative, with which the therapist aims to help through a co-authorship, in navigating these ambiguities, is an intellectual task that the ego can metabolize. Much unlike the bombardment with contradiction and noise, that dissolves identity rather than strengthening it. The low-grade confusion that the ego is constantly facing in the endless turns and bends of the self-help economy just recycles the individual's problems, for another round of marketing bombardment. This has nothing to do with the *identity crisis* Erikson (1959) identifies as the suspended state of inner tension, from a reorganizing psychic system. And most of all, as we will later be able to conclude, *this* is deliberate.

Each piece of advice is issued in isolation in this jungle of competing imperatives, designed for mass application and of course with no narrative frame. And ends in a dead-end road. While one influencer insists discipline is the key to self-respect, the next spiritual coach urges self-compassion is the only true foundation of all healing. The new non-fictional bestseller urges hard workouts before 5 a.m. but TikTok's most viral fitness guru has discovered more sleep as the secret weapon. While none of these are harmful in and of themselves, their simultaneous availability can create despair. Of course, there is no external reference for hierarchy, context, validation. Because all of them are true. All of them have their acclaim, their praise and their endless testimonials. All of them are the best.

And yet again, it is not the advice that is false. It is the psychological fragmentation in an individual with no guidance, that can not be reconciled at the level of reason. The subject has no principled ground from which to assess its relevance to their particular psychic situation. And this over-saturation of best versions disables the stable sense that one's feelings and judgments are made from an inner authority that guides. This is the exact opposite of what Winnicott (1960) described as essential for psychological growth, where the self must perceive and locate itself as the source of feeling and decision, as opposed to reactive and *borrowed*. In its absence, Winnicott (ibid.) warned, there might develop a *false self*: one that is structurally designed to comply and manage external demands – and becomes deeply ill and dissatisfied. It is functionally *un*-alive.

This structural problem in endless self-help paradigms disables the subject from reflecting, but lets them only evermore compare. The psyche is a switching station caught between protocols, guides and templates – all of which essential, critical – and corrodes. Voices, ever louder, ever more glittering, confident and authoritative, exacerbate this sense of confusion that would only be natural. The subject, in the fading sense of self-knowledge, begins to distrust the confusion *itself*: 'Am I resisting growth or is it (my) right to reject this framework?'. And if the constant tension between voices and all the sprinkle is *not* a problem and leads *not* to narrative fatigue and collapse, then why does it not work..? No, it is a problem. Because the individual loses not only the sense of what is right for them, but also the ability to even know that they have the right to ask.

This affective reality of paralysis stands in stark contrast to real agency. The array of contradictory techniques and motivational credos is all but liberation. What Giddens (1991) calls 'reflexive modernity' is the obligation to endlessly make choices, and then revise them, justify them and personalize them further. In place of a stable narrative arc, the individual becomes solely responsible for the assembly of their identity from fragments, each of which promises ultimate clarity, none offering closure. This is paradoxical because the more available *best* choices, the more insecurity is effectively created. The service is indecision. Erich Fromm (1941), long preceding the digital age and modern self-help culture, saw that the subject confronted with too much freedom ends in despair. The responsibility and uncertainty that comes with it, according to Fromm, has the subject respond with anxiety instead of agency, becoming paralysed and retreat into dependency. Because it offers structure.

The performance of freedom under these conditions is practically identical with what Fromm meant when he elegantly distinguished *freedom from* and *freedom to*, of which modernity failed to equip the individual with the latter. They are liberated from external constraints, which at first glance is positive. But the ultimate freedom *to* is actually a void. No certainties, no orientation, no grounding. And this exact freedom, according to Fromm, is experienced as disorientation. The modern market of self-help literature, contradictory gurus and other formats is devoid of shared and stable coordinates, uncontainable. It crushes the consumer under the weight of responsibility to choose the right path out of right paths, and while demanding autonomy, the consumer is not *ready* for autonomous decisions – because they have to optimize, curate. Thus, they easily submit to new authorities, blindly, or even lash out – mechanisms Fromm termed 'escapes from freedom'.

And what is experienced by the individual as existential despair, is just rebranded by the market as the 'journey': you, being searching, is right for you. It is the learning process. It makes you grow. The exhaustion you feel is not systemic, by the structural design, it is because you are still not complete; but of course we are supporting you with the right tools to find the missing parts. Doubt is not your signal to rest but to be overcome. Compulsion dressed as choice.

Consequently, what happens is a perpetual epistemic disorientation. And I want to highlight that this is not because of the momentary contradiction or uncertainty, nor is it because of the incapable individual. Epistemic disorientation, in this context, is the state in which the capacity to organize knowledge and insight into a usable psychological structure begins to fail: the erosion of any contextual anchor that would allow the psyche to metabolize meaning. Everything arrives without scale or epistemic cues, all truths claim the same urgency, all voices perform the same level of authority. The result is a collapse of semantic weight. Everything matters equally, and therefore nothing does. Meaning-processing systems can no longer operate in stability, frameworks dissolve into each other too quickly to even take shape.

In a map with no legend, movement is real, but direction is gone.

Part II

The Psychopolitics of Responsibility and Inadequacy

3 THE COMMAND TO OPTIMIZE: FROM POSSIBILITY TO ONTOLOGICAL IMPERATIVE

3.1 Agency and Moral Coercion. 'You Can' Becomes 'You Must'.

The cultural, or: cult-logic of the self-help paradigm has hardened the mere possibility of becoming into an ontological mandate. The idea that one can grow has pretty much always been part of existence. But in the realms we are exploring, it has metastasized into a demand; one *must*. Without being literal about it, the urgency of self-improvement has been moralized. Self-encounter, stillness and uncertainty are not in the DNA of this paradigm.

Far from a linguistic accident, this is a revaluation of being itself. In original philosophical register, possibility implied an openness toward the horizon of potential; something healthy, neither guaranteed, nor required. It is simply there. In existential thought, growth is the meaningful act within the constraints of finitude and choice (Sartre, 1943/2018); grounded essentially in freedom; the opposite of obligation. Clinical perspectives regard change as emergent in conflict and mourning, and assembled through the labor of symbolization. Willpower alone is not sufficient (cf. Freud, 1923/1961; cf. Chapter 1.2). These are theoretical anchors that shall help understand how far the modern mindset-cult has moved away from seminal thoughts of growth and choice. In the modern machinery, growth is abused as the condition of continued worth. The neoliberal subject goes through a pivotal distortion in their subjective value, that is strongly conditional upon upward motion. The grammar of growth has changed into an imperative.

Unfortunately, this logic is not confined to pop-spirituality and coaching circles (anymore). It has infiltrated even those zones once tasked with preserving psychological integrity. Nowadays the lines between psychological rigor and pop-culture are continuously blurring. And so it comes that therapy manuals, emergent regulation techniques and compassion guides echo an optimization language: heal, build resilience, move on. You get the impression that you are always behind your pursued self. And that brings about the experience that the own being is insufficient unless it is in transformation. One that can be measured and tracked, see previous chapters. The inability to live up to ever-present imperative standards to become more can crush the neoliberal subject; the neurotic subject of the past has become the depressive subject of the present (Ehrenberg, 2010).

In essence, the offer remains a form of freedom. But this freedom is essentially a veneer when seen in the context of modern language. You still hear the rhetoric of possibility but with a morally coercive undertone. As mentioned before, the scene defines the meaning. And even though the choice of words is still careful, encouraging, the relentless stream of how good you *could be* has stigmatizing effects. After all, who is to blame if you refuse every offer? You had the choice, in abundance. Why didn't you choose. You shall not become who you are but become better, and better never ends. And that is ontological violence.

It may have been a developmental byproduct of the market, that it has become such an ideological structure. But in the contemporary doctrine of self-optimization mindsets, inaction is no longer neutral. The refusal to act is not interpreted in context or contemplation, but as a deficiency marker; of character. In a system where every action is framed as a choice and every choice reflects the self, non-action *can* only signify failure. As improvement is always available – in a new book, a video, a mindest course – the mere existence of access renders its non-use suspect. Welcome to the *you could have society*. What does it say about you and your ambition that you haven't? This is how agency becomes coercive (violent) in that ability morphs into mandate and its refusal is made evidence of your personal failure. And the motive of internalization is of course still in operation: you *have* not only failed, you *are* a failure. Because your act reflects your identity.

But inaction is not equal to an avoidance pattern. We should keep that in mind. However, the subject, saturated in therapeutic language but severed from therapeutic context (or expertise) learns to self-indict in the absence of movement. When hesitation to submit yourself to the mindset standard is resistance, and resistance is a flaw, then the verdict is already rendered. Of course no one needs to question, as resistance is no longer an unconscious defense to be explored and understood. You had the choice to become perfect but refused – so don't complain. Toxic positivity in essence.

The obliteration of nuance is a logical consequence: you are required to reinterpret your own hesitation as a misalignment that must be fixed, not a message to be heard. Interpretation is not existent in the binary world of labels: you act and succeed or you stall and rot. There is no idle state, an 'in-between', where genuine psychological work happens, is obliterated.

Lastly, potentiality is now a moral duty. Potential, once a horizon or a realm of what might be, now represents a mechanism of inner debt. Even momentarily, it is unethical to remain as one is. All hypothetical versions of the self that went unpursued are adding to the escalating bill the individual has to justify before their inner tribunal. They are guilty of underperformance against an imagined self. Culpable for the gap between who they are and who they might be instead.

Except, there is no redemption; there cannot be. Because in emotional capitalism, your horizon, your potential, escalates continually – throwing you into paralysis and trapping you in ontological insufficiency.

3.2 Homo Oeconomicus, of the Soul

When the human psyche becomes a product in development, emotions are only soft data. Insight in the form of an internal UX feedback makes emotional shortcomings pivot points of an early-stage enterprise. It is volatile, aspirational, in constant need of iteration. The logic of a start-up is imported into psychic life. A self that is launched, not lived. Just like clinical language is no longer reserved for clinical psychology, economic language is colonized for the affirmative new paradigm of personhood. All that you *are*, every bit of you is thought and spoken of as an asset for greater purpose and you must not fail to utilize it. Return on the inner investment must always be visible and demonstrable. A structural mutation of the individual, as Foucault (2008/1978) anticipated long before the age of social networks and highlight reels. As he argued, the subject is now responsible for their own capacity of generating value – *neoliberal governmentality*. The condition of freedom is that you now must produce your own adequacy. The reason I find the analogy of a start-up well-fitting is that the volatility and the proneness to collapse is inherent to the speculative nature. Nowadays, it is valorized as a heroic model not only of business, but of *being*, sold daily across thousands of thumbnails, podcast intros, pseudo-psychological and -philosophical bestseller covers. The spirit of modern capitalism requires the subject to become a project without completion, disembedded from place, history and inner structure (Boltanski & Chiapello, 2005). Your sovereign self has to be unburdened, by contradiction, by anything virtually. The industry sells an alignment with the system that broke you in the first place, but does not care about why modern life is so unlivable for so many. Actually, modern life is wonderful, and if it is not for you, then your mindset is not right. It is an easy equation. You have simply not yet decided to become the 'best version of yourself'; richer, smarter, better looking, a *brand*.

Meanwhile, those who sell these ideologies are rarely what they pretend to be. They are, in many cases, broken by the same forces, just better at monetizing their breakdown (cf. Gross, 2024b). It is a systemic impossibility that there are only winners and that a strategy works for everybody. There is an abundance of individuals getting out of this machinery and speaking out about how fake the market actually is. The exhaustion, however, is only felt after the impactful realization comes that the tools and frameworks the industry so aggressively pushes are only a mere illusion. No one can become a fully managed being. No psyche can maintain permanent 'upskilling', you can not *plan* your way into inner peace according to a step-by-step schedule. Human beings do not function like a roadmap, or an app. The human being mourns. It collapses. It loves in ways that make no sense. And that is not a defect of the system – it is the system. It is what makes us human.

What we actually know, but have been gaslit into forgetting is: highlight reels do not accurately display human lives.

The ultimate violent act of the self-help ethos is the manufacture of emotional debt: not only are you required to improve, but you are made to believe that you owe it to yourself. Your inner peace, your stillness, your grief, are framed not as sacred terrain, but as unpaid invoices. This is not selfmastery. It is servitude disguised as autonomy. It is the lifeline of an industry that capitalizes on the sustained insufficiency that it creates. Just because there are imaginary versions of a 'better self' does neither mean they must, or should even, be pursued, nor that they will provide any healing to a fractured soul. We *do not owe, and are not owed*, perpetual improvement. What we are owed is space to be unremarkable, unproductive and whole. Living a life that is neither optimized nor explained, but felt – that may be the most radical act of all.

3.3   Fantasy of Equal Potential.   Structural Reality Erased

As one of the foundational architectures of the self-help industry is *positive thinking*, there must also be the presumption that there is something to think positively of. In a euphoric denial of reality, it comes down to the complete denial of structural and systemic reality. The idea of everyone starting from the same place distributes responsibility equally. But this is a fundamental misconception, or rather a lie.

We are not all equal in origin and we are not all equally responsible for the 'outcome'. The ideological spine of every seminar, every book, every course, is that success happens through willpower (i.e., your mindset). Thus, if that fantasy fails, it you who must answer for the gap.

But the real world is not equal. It is structured – by class, race, geography, trauma, access, inheritance. Some are born into networks, generational wealth, education and cultural safety. Others are born into survival. And no, *not* only in the third world. And to pretend otherwise is moral bankruptcy. While start-up prophets and entrepreneurial mindset gurus preach that anyone can do anything, the Bezoses und Musks of the world do not represent possibility. These exceptions are not evidence anyone can make it. Inheritance, privilege and *luck* are not something that is achievable. Nor does it have anything to do with mindset or willpower. But exactly this is what erodes clinical realities just as well: one cannot out-journal childhood neglect and reframe systemic poverty or optimize their way out of attachment trauma.

In other words: self-help economy cannot co-exist with structural awareness. It strongly depends on erasing the difference between limitation and laziness. It *must* deny all distinctions between opportunity and privilege. And therefore, it can never afford to acknowledge the deep embedding of suffering.

Byung-Chul Han (2015) diagnoses the neoliberal subject with a self-exploitation in the name of inner freedom – we are not forbidden but invited. We are not punished, but motivated; however, the result is no less punishing. Telling someone that they can make it, because everybody can, with disregard to the reality that they can in fact *not*, is a weaponization of freedom, is not an infinite horizon but a Fata Morgana.

3.4 How Toxic Positivity Fosters Pathogenic Repression

The affective logic of modern mindset coaching malpractice and self-help guru culture is centered around a narrow corridor of permitted and desirable states – all of them bright, productive and terminally upbeat. This amounts to toxic positivity because it attempts to render necessary human feelings obsolete, unwanted and better if *not felt*. This censorship of emotions trains the subject to feel only selectively, which has consequences. It has clinical and existential impact.

Long has psychology known that repression of disavowed emotion does not eliminate it, it does not vanish, but it returns; in disguise. As psychic unrest, symbolic. Freud (1926) had already recognized that repression resolves no inner conflict but has a disintegrative force, ripping through coherence and producing symptoms. When negative affect is denied, compulsively, deliberately, and upon instruction, the psyche loses its expressivity and the self loses access to inner dialogue and understanding. And exactly there lies the danger of toxic positivity: it misinterprets reality and actively trains the subject away from integration. Ill-informed mindset coaching practices that attempt to 'redirect' do instead overwrite. And these are not 'tools' for healing but instead, in clinical terms, pathogenic defense mechanisms – they mask emotional displacement as progress. Consequently, these instructions to suppress disable the ego's capacity to integrate experience, which over time leads to fragmentation and unresolved tension.

This is not to say that an individual reading a self-help

58

book will end up in pathogenic repression. It is a warning that the functional intelligence of affect itself is systematically neglected in an economy whose lifeline is the enforced positivity that the subject does not feel – this severs the connection of the consumer from their own regulatory capacities, and thereby worsens the situation, potentially. As Fuchs (2018) argues, affect is not an obstacle but is necessary for the self to cohere over time. It must not be bypassed, it must be inhabited in its full spectrum, including these uncomfortable spaces where they are dwelling in what is not yet resolved. Ahmed (2010) shows how the contemporary culture of mindset coaching and toxic positive affirmations do exactly the opposite: the problem is not happiness, but that its pursuit is conditional on obedience to affective norms the discourse prescribes. After all, it is inarguably unhealthy to censor and overwrite emotions and deem them undesirable, because the psyche resists this. Eventually, reframing stops working. Gratitude patterns falter.

It is to feel what must be felt.

3.5   Gradually Becoming What One Never Wanted

No human being wakes up with the sudden desire or goal to optimize their calendar. No one in despair cries out for a twelve-week system, and no crisis begins with the wish to become ones 'own CEO'. However, in the self-help economy, these appear as the ultimate and obvious truths, as default aspirations. You might not have known, but you have always wanted that. These Trojan horses are simply imported because the *seem to make sense*. There is however a specific kind of suffering that emerges from unexamined goals one carries: ones that were never freely chosen and emerged from a sense of lack or an inner aspiration, original and genuine, but that have been culturally enforced. Silently adopted (Plesa, 2021). And that happens before you can even contemplate *why* you are unfulfilled. The answer precedes the question – convenient. You're given a replacement before you know what you have lost. And so begins a new psychological captivity with *borrowed meaning* (Han, 2017); you want things that you never knew you wanted. And you work towards new motivations that are empowering – until they are not.

Own values, aspirations and deep longing is not important, because the default solutions sit waiting, and the ideal life has already been scripted. Whether or not that fits personal history or biography is less important. Financial freedom is something good, hard to argue. But still, they often emerge not from depth but have simply been rehearsed from the discourse so very often that they appear natural, self-evident. Why would you question eating healthy and being financially independent (cf. Illouz, 2007)? It makes sense to want that.

Where this becomes the most obvious is health-branch of the cult – and for a reason. Behind the wellness-tinted optimism lies a radical shift in moral architecture that is unique to the health mindset industry. Where other branches rely on the narrative of passive inadequacy, the healthbranch capitalizes on the anxiety of direct negative physical consequence. In other words, biologically framed self-harm. You are not only failing to optimize but actively damaging yourself. Health becomes a weaponized ideal, the body is used for blackmail. I am not talking of classic addictions, or other destructive habits where suitable health advice would be appropriate – the new moral pressure bends to an inward axis, and focuses on *inaction*. Your body will be your witness and judge; your inflammation, your fatigue, your cortisol, your cellular aging. You have been warned, by biohacking influencers, longevity podcasts and diet coaches, and sooner or later, you will pay the price for your willful neglect. Knowledge is now an indictment (cf. Canguilhem, 1991). You are poisoning yourself with each bit of sugar, and your body's biology is silently ruined by all the small failures every day. And you should know better.

And yet, so very many subjects collapse after their period
of intense optimization. And not because self-optimization always fails. They may even reach the pre-scripted goals. But
they were never the ones that emerged from their own space.
It is not that the goal was too hard, but it was never theirs.
Authentic direction begins elsewhere. Because sometimes,
there is simply no goal at all. But it takes sovereignty to
refuse a systemic goal. And, in relation to the health dogma,
I could not have found a better description than Per-Einar
Binder's (2022) *Suffering a Healthy Life.*

After all, goals not chosen yourself are new chains painted
in gold.

4 Sufficiency and Psychological Depth: A Reclamation

4.1 An Ethical Imperative

To reclaim psychological depth is not a theoretical task, but an ethical obligation. In a climate where affect is commodified, with monetized routines and inner life chopped into bite-sized deliverables, I see the refusal to reduce the psyche to performance as an act of due resistance. And also as a restoration of understanding of care.

No, the human mind was never designed to be 'efficient'. Its complexity is not a problem that must be solved. Clinical integrity is to make room for ambiguity and contradiction, for delay and regression. It is precisely the *reason* why it is sacred, because it resists the monetization all around it – and it does not 'transform better' the more force is applied. But depth is endangered in this day and age, where everything must follow the pulse of the algorithm, and suffering meaningfully, as a sign of psychological work, is substandard. Where the self-help cult sells strategy, psychology shall offer presence. Where reassurance is proclaimed, it shall offer truth. And where outcomes are the label, psychology shall reestablish the dignity of process, without measurement.

This is not nostalgia for outdated theory – but a defense of *moral realism*. Suffering cannot be 'hacked', it cannot be

62

bypassed through the right self-affirming slogans and it cannot be displaced without cost. When we flatten affect into mood states or teach people that negative emotion is a malfunction that is not only a sign of failure but must be adjusted to the paradigm, we do much more than miseducate: it is a violation of the ethical contract of psychological speech. It is telling people that they are broken for being human. The task is not to innovate but to protect and hold. The traditions of depth psychology – Freud's demand for slowness, Jung's radical embrace of psychic multiplicity, Winnicott's space for non-doing – were all ethical stances that refuse to distort suffering into something marketable.

The modern individual navigating the self-help industry is lost in advice and also abandoned by truth. And that is by design, because the system gaslights them into believing that their innate complexity is the problem to get rid of, where it is the very feat that is to be understood. But blinded by contradictions, and surrounded by *best* approaches, vulnerability is fertile ground to sustain a running system fueled by pain.

You are allowed not to be improving.

4.2 The Refusal of Instrumental Affect

To feel without function has become a forgotten human freedom in a culture where the sheer fact of feeling is no longer enough. What if the insistence on use is itself the very thing that hollows emotional life? The stance this work has is that not all experience must be converted into outcome. Not all wounds and fractures of the soul must be turning points that can be utilized and not all anger and sadness must be targeted. In that regard, the refusal of instrumental affect is a reinstallation of mystery in the human experience. It says: I will not mine my sadness, repackage my anxiety, drag my grief into a frame. I will let it be heavy, disorganized and contradictory. Because that is where it is most honest, where it can be experienced, without a guise.

The ethical relation, according to philosopher Emmanuel

Levinas (1969), begins when we learn to encounter another not as a use-case but as a *face*: perceive them as a presence that has no utility. If we drive that, in the refusal to allow the most human elements of psychology be co-opted by optimization markets, we treat our own sadness as relative to ourselves, instead of a task to be completed.

And most importantly, this refusal does not at all interrupt healing, but it makes it possible in the first place. A process with no script. Bearing a feeling without using it gives it the space it needs to be understood, and gives you the time to let it speak to you (Tamir & Ford, 2012).

4.3 Psychological and Political Philosophy of 'Being Enough'

To say *I am enough* is not an affirmation in this context, but a confrontation. It confronts a culture whose survival depends on permanent dissatisfaction. It denies a system that offers no finish line. Being enough silences an inner voice that has been rehearsed and monetized, and that insists you must be better and more. To say enough does not contradict growth, but it can be seen as a redefinition of what growth actually means when it is not governed by shame. Because in psychological terms, 'enoughness' is not a state of completion: it should be seen as a mode of relating to the self that does not position value elsewhere. It should be the end of exile from the present condition of being.

Politically, the self-help and mindset industry borrow from neoliberal capitalism, and thereby depend on the subject's inner unrest and its sustenance. Such systems can, by design, not metabolize inner peace. Contentment would always be a contradiction to its lifeline, because who does not feel broken does not buy the cure. And yet, paradoxically, even 'I am enough' has been conquered by the very marketplace it should actually dismantle. It is a mantra that decorates book covers, tattoos, mugs. But in this form, it is sold as declaration. It functions as an assignment; you must feel *enough* to qualify as healed, you must *embody* it. It still contains the possibility of failure. Even being enough is turned into a strategy, as an optimization of your current self. But the very point of being enough is that it does not have to be proven, including to the self. It is not a feeling, not a mindset.

Much rather, it is a complete withdrawal from the race. Inhabitance of the psychic room where there is not *asked* whether you feel enough. Where there is no preparation. It is simple existence with no apology, no explanation and *no possibility* to fail at being enough. Against the violence of striving, being enough, in a sense of depth psychology, is not a voice that continuously whispers 'you are perfect', but it says 'You are here. And being is worth, and it is whole.'

BIBLIOGRAPHY

Abidin, C. (2016). "Aren't These Just Young, Rich Women Doing Vain Things Online?": Influencer Selfies as Subversive Frivolity. Social Media + Society, 2(2).

Ahmed, S. (2010). The Promise of Happiness. Duke University Press.

Ahmed, S. (2014). The cultural politics of emotion (2nd ed.). Edinburgh University Press.

Aristotle. (2007). Rhetoric (W. Rhys Roberts, Trans.). Dover Publications. (Original work published ca. 350 B.C.E.)

Baudrillard, J. (1994). Simulacra and simulation (S. F. Glaser, Trans.). University of Michigan Press.

Berlant, L. (2011). Cruel optimism. Duke University Press.

Binder, P.-E. (2022). Suffering a healthy life-On the existential dimension of health. Frontiers in Psychology, 13, Article 803792.

Bollas, C. (1987). The shadow of the object: Psychoanalysis of the unthought known. Columbia University Press.

Boltanski, L., & Chiapello, È. (2005). The new spirit of capitalism (G. Elliott, Trans.). Verso.

Bourdieu, P. (1991). Language and symbolic power (J. B. Thompson, Ed.). Harvard University Press.

Buber, M. (2000). I and Thou (R. G. Smith, Trans.). Scribner. (Original work published 1937)

Cabanas, E., & Illouz, E. (2019). Manufacturing Happy Citizens: How the Science and Industry of Happiness Control Our Lives. Polity.

Canguilhem, G. (1991). The normal and the pathological (C. R. Fawcett, Trans.). Zone Books. (Original work published 1943)

Crary, J. (2013). 24/7: Late capitalism and the ends of sleep. Verso.

Dobson, A. S. (2015). Postfeminist digital cultures: Femininity, social media, and selfrepresentation. Palgrave Macmillan.

Ehrenberg, A. (2010). The weariness of the self: Diagnosing the history of depression in the contemporary age. McGill-Queen's University Press.

Ehrenreich, B. (2009). Bright-Sided: How Positive Thinking Is Undermining America. Metropolitan.

Erikson, E. H. (1959). Identity and the life cycle. International Universities Press.

Filho, F. A., Rosa, P. O., & Marchiori, G. (2020). From homo oeconomicus to the performance subject: The trajectory of the subject in the neoliberal model in the thoughts of Foucault and Byung-Chul Han. Research, Society and Development, 9(9), 130942964.

Foucault, M. (1980). Power/knowledge: Selected interviews and other writings, 1972-1977 (C. Gordon, Ed.). Pantheon Books.

Foucault, M. (2008). The birth of biopolitics: Lectures at the Collège de France, 1978-1979 (G. Burchell, Trans.). Palgrave Macmillan.

Freud, S. (1926). Inhibitions, symptoms and anxiety. In J. Strachey, & A. Freud (Eds.), The standard edition of the complete psychological works of Sigmund Freud (pp. 77-175). London: The Hogarth Press.

Freud, S. (1957). Mourning and melancholia. In The standard edition of the complete psychological works of Sigmund Freud (Vol. 14, pp. 243-258). Hogarth Press. (Original work published 1917)

Freud, S. (1961). The ego and the id (J. Strachey, Trans.). W. W. Norton. (Original work published 1923)

Freud, S. (1961). The ego and the id. W W Norton & Co.

Fromm, E. (1941). Escape from freedom. Farrar & Rinehart.

Fuchs, T. (2018). Ecology of the brain: The phenomenology and biology of the embodied mind. Oxford University Press.

Furedi, F. (2004). Therapy culture: Cultivating vulnerability in an uncertain age. Routledge.

Galtung, J. (1969). Violence, peace, and peace research. Journal of Peace Research, 6(3), 167-191.

Garde-Hansen, J., & Gorton, K. (2013). Emotion online: Theorizing affect on the internet. Palgrave Macmillan.

Giddens, A. (1991). Modernity and Self-Identity: Self and Society in the Late Modern Age. Stanford University Press.

Gill, R., & Orgad, S. (2018). The Amazing Bounce-Backable Woman: Resilience and the Psychological Turn in Neoliberalism. Sociological Research Online, 23(2), 477-495.

Gillespie, T. (2018). Custodians of the internet: Platforms, content moderation, and the hidden decisions that shape social media. Yale University Press.

Goffman, E. (1959). The presentation of self in everyday life.

68

Anchor Books.

Gross, T. (2024a). Cognitive Nemesis: A Psychological Synthesis. Minkowski Institute Press.

Gross, T. (2024b). Dopamine Machine: The Neuropsychological Cost of Escalating Social Approval. Minkowski Institute Press.

Hamann, T. H. (2009). Neoliberalism, governmentality, and ethics. Foucault Studies, (6), 37-59.

Han, B.-C. (2015). The burnout society (E. Butler, Trans.). Stanford University Press. (Original work published 2010)

Han, B.-C. (2017). Psychopolitics: Neoliberalism and New Technologies of Power. Verso.
Huibers, M. J., & Wessely, S. (2006). The act of diagnosis: pros and cons of labelling chronic fatigue syndrome. Psychological medicine, 36(7), 895-900.

Illouz, E. (2007). Cold intimacies: The making of emotional capitalism. Polity.

Illouz, E. (2008). Saving the modern soul: Therapy, emotions, and the culture of self-help. University of California Press.

Laplanche, J., & Pontalis, J.-B. (1973). The language of psycho-analysis (D. Nicholson-Smith, Trans.). W. W. Norton.

Laub, D. (1992). Bearing witness, or the vicissitudes of listening. In S. Felman & D. Laub (Eds.), Testimony: Crises of witnessing in literature, psychoanalysis, and history (pp. 57-74). Routledge.

Levay, C., Jönsson, J., & Huzzard, T. (2020). Quantified Control in Healthcare Work: Suggestions for Future Research. Wiley-Blackwell: Financial Accountability & Management in Governments.

Levinas, E. (1969). Totality and infinity: An essay on exteriority (A. Lingis, Trans.). Duquesne University Press.

Lupton, D. (2016). The Quantified Self: A Sociology of Self-Tracking. (First ed.) Polity Press.

McAdams, D. P. (1993). The stories we live by: Personal myths and the making of the self. Guilford Press.

Ogden, T. H. (1994). Subjects of analysis. Karnac Books.

Parker, M. (2010). Diagnosis, power and certainty: Response to Davis. Journal of Bioethical Inquiry, 7(3), 291-297.

Plesa, P. (2021). Reassessing existential constructs and subjectivity: Freedom and authenticity in neoliberalism. Journal of Humanistic Psychology.

Rimke, H. M. (2000). Governing citizens through self-help literature. Cultural Studies, 14(1), 6178.

Rogers, C. R. (1957). The necessary and sufficient conditions of therapeutic personality change. Journal of Consulting Psychology, 21(2), 95-103.

Rose, N. (1999). Governing the soul: The shaping of the private self (2nd ed.). Free Association Books.

Rose, N. (1999). Powers of freedom: Reframing political thought. Cambridge University Press.

Rosenfield, S. (1997). Labeling mental illness: The effects of received services and perceived stigma on life satisfaction. American Sociological Review, 62(4), 660-672.

Sartre, J.-P. (2018). Being and Nothingness: An Essay in Phenomenological Ontology (S. Richmond, Trans.; 1st ed.). Routledge.

Schüll, N. D. (2016). Addiction by Design: Machine Gambling in Las Vegas. Princeton University Press.

Searle, J. R. (1975). A Taxonomy of Illocutionary Acts. In

K. Gunderson (ed.), Language, Mind and Knowledge (p./pp. 344-369). University of Minnesota Press.

Stolorow, R. D., Atwood, G. E., & Brandchaft, B. (Eds.). (1994). The intersubjective perspective. Jason Aronson.

Tamir, M., & Ford, B. Q. (2012). When feeling bad is expected to be good: emotion regulation and outcome expectancies in social conflicts. Emotion (Washington, D.C.), 12(4), 807-816.

Wachtel, P. L. (2008). Relational theory and the practice of psychotherapy. The Guilford Press.

Wampold B. E. (2015). How important are the common factors in psychotherapy? An update. World psychiatry : official journal of the World Psychiatric Association (WPA), 14(3), 270-277.

White, M. (2017). Big Data, Algorithms, and Quantification. In: The Decline of the Individual. Palgrave Macmillan, Cham.

Winnicott, D. W. (1960). Ego distortion in terms of true and false self. In The maturational processes and the facilitating environment (pp. 140-152). Hogarth Press.

Winnicott, D. W. (1965). The maturational processes and the facilitating environment. Hogarth Press.

Wittgenstein, L. (1953). Philosophical investigations (G. E. M. Anscombe, Trans.). WileyBlackwell.

Yu, P. (2023). Self as enterprise: The subjectivity in Foucault's biopolitics. Lecture Notes in Education Psychology and Public Media.

Zuboff, S. (2019). The age of surveillance capitalism. Profile Books.

www.ingramcontent.com/pod-product-compliance
Lightning Source LLC
Chambersburg PA
CBHW052105270326
41931CB00012B/2889